# A Closer Look at the

# ANIMAL
# KINGDOM

# A Closer Look at the
# ANIMAL
# KINGDOM

### Edited by Sherman Hollar

Britannica®
Educational Publishing

IN ASSOCIATION WITH

ROSEN
EDUCATIONAL SERVICES

Published in 2012 by Britannica Educational Publishing
(a trademark of Encyclopædia Britannica, Inc.)
in association with Rosen Educational Services, LLC
29 East 21st Street, New York, NY 10010.

Distributed exclusively by Rosen Educational Services.
For a listing of additional Britannica Educational Publishing titles, call toll free (800) 237-9932.

First Edition

Britannica Educational Publishing
Michael I. Levy: Executive Editor, Encyclopædia Britannica
J.E. Luebering: Director, Core Reference Group, Encyclopædia Britannica
Adam Augustyn: Assistant Manager, Encyclopædia Britannica

Anthony L. Green: Editor, Compton's by Britannica
Michael Anderson: Senior Editor, Compton's by Britannica
Sherman Hollar: Associate Editor, Compton's by Britannica

Marilyn L. Barton: Senior Coordinator, Production Control
Steven Bosco: Director, Editorial Technologies
Lisa S. Braucher: Senior Producer and Data Editor
Yvette Charboneau: Senior Copy Editor
Kathy Nakamura: Manager, Media Acquisition

Rosen Educational Services
Alexandra Hanson-Harding: Editor
Nelson Sá: Art Director
Cindy Reiman: Photography Manager
Matthew Cauli: Designer, Cover Design
Introduction by Alexandra Hanson-Harding

**Library of Congress Cataloging-in-Publication Data**

A closer look at the animal kingdom / edited by Sherman Hollar.
    p. cm.—(Introduction to biology)
"In association with Britannica Educational Publishing, Rosen Educational Services."
Includes bibliographical references and index.
ISBN 978-1-61530-531-5 (library binding)
1. Animals—Classification—Juvenile literature.  I. Hollar, Sherman.
QL351.C59 2012
590.1'2—dc22

2011010406

*Manufactured in the United States of America*

**On the cover:** An elephant, the largest living land animal, is seen against the sweeping background at
Kilimanjaro, northern Tanzania, Africa. *Shutterstock.com.*

Interior background images Shutterstock.com.

# CONTENTS

Animals are everywhere. Even busy New York City, full of cars and concrete, is teeming with animal life. Ants march up a sidewalk. Pigeons peck at crumbs, while squirrels search for nuts. A horse drawing a carriage trots by Boston terriers dragging their owner to the dog park. A gray rat skitters across subway tracks while a cat stares down from a skyscraper at tiny taxis and people below. No matter where you live, you will be surrounded by animals—including human beings! This book will help you learn more about your fellow members of the animal kingdom.

There are more than ten million kinds of animals in the world, and about 1.3 million have been identified by scientists. All life forms started in the same place: in the oceans some 3.5 billion years ago. Our common ancestors were simple single-celled organisms. Over time, many living things became more complex as they adapted to various environments. Multicellular organisms began to form and separate into different species as they moved. Some moved into freshwater, others to land.

Members of the kingdom Animalia are different from all other living things on Earth. We are eukaryotes, which means that our cells have various complex parts such as a nucleus and organelles. (Bacteria and archaea are made up of simpler prokaryotic cells.) But unlike plants, which are also eukaryotes, we cannot make our own food through the process of photosynthesis—animals must rely on eating vegetation and other animals to survive. Animals are metazoans (the prefix *meta-* means many) because they are made of many cells. (Single-celled animal-like creatures are called protozoa.)

Scientists who study animal life classify animals based on their bodies. That helps scientists decide how animals are related to others. One of the most important ways of classifying animals is by whether they are invertebrates (who lack a backbone) or vertebrates (who have one). Invertebrates make up 95 percent of animal species. The first animals were invertebrates, such as sponges and jellyfish. About 85 percent of invertebrates are arthropods (the word means "jointed foot"). Many arthropods have an exoskeleton made of a substance called

Cygnets (baby swans) walk in the rain at Abbotsbury Swannery in Weymouth, England. The swannery is home to a herd of 800 wild swans. Matt Cardy/Getty Images

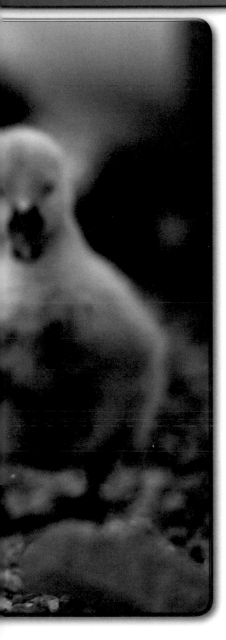

chitin. Arthropods include centipedes, spiders, scorpions, and lobsters. Most significantly, they include insects. More than one million insect species have been identified—the largest group within the animal kingdom.

Vertebrates are animals with backbones. Some live in the sea, such as fish; others live on land; others, like birds, take to the air. They make up only about 5 percent of all animal species. The complexity of their bodies lets vertebrates have bigger, more complex brains. The most advanced vertebrates are mammals. Only 5,000 species of mammals exist. The blue whale is a mammal that is the largest living

9

creature on Earth. It can grow to be more than 100 feet (30 meters) long and weight 300,000 pounds (136,000 kilograms).

Scientists also study how animals adapt to their environments. While some animals are solitary, others are more social. Bees live in hives. Wolves live in packs. Some build homes. Groundhogs live in complex underground burrows with connecting tunnels. Other animals have adapted themselves to live with humans, such as our closest companions, dogs.

No doubt about it, animals large and small—including us—adapt themselves to survive in many different ways. This volume will help you to understand and identify the animals that live around you—whether you're in a bustling city, a quiet suburb, or out in the country—and those that populate our planet.

# CHAPTER 1

# THE VARIETY OF ANIMAL LIFE

Living things are divided into three main groups called domains. Single-celled organisms called bacteria and archaea each constitute their own domain. All other organisms make up a third domain, Eukarya, which includes not only single-celled algae and protozoa but also animals and other multicellular organisms. Animals form the largest group within the Eukarya. They range from very simple invertebrates, such as sponges, to highly complex mammals, such as whales, monkeys, and humans. Animals display some key differences that distinguish them from other living things. For example, what is the difference between an animal such as a horse and a plant such as grass? A horse moves around in the pasture eating grass. It trots toward you when you offer it a lump of sugar and reacts favorably when you stroke its head. The grass, however, is rooted to one place. It does not respond behaviorally to people or to the horse in any

*A horse eats grass in Oxfordshire, England.* Tim Graham Photo Library/Getty Images

way. More importantly, plants use nutrients from the soil and chemical reactions from the sun to make their own food. This process is called photosynthesis. Animals cannot make their own food—to survive, they have to eat plants or other animals.

Scientists estimate that there may be more than ten million different kinds of animals on Earth today. About 1.3 million kinds have been identified to date, and new kinds are continually being discovered. In the seas, from the surface down to the black depths where no ray of light penetrates, on mountaintops and in deserts, in mud and in hot pools, some form of animal life may be found.

Animals are extremely varied in form, size, and habits. The smallest animals, such as the crustaceans called copepods, are so tiny that they can barely be seen without a microscope. The largest, the blue whales, may be more than 100 feet (30 meters) long and weigh 300,000 pounds (136,000 kilograms).

Some of the most familiar animals, such as dogs, birds, frogs, and fish, have a backbone and a central nervous system. They are called vertebrates, meaning animals with spinal columns or backbones. Animals without backbones are called invertebrates and include arthropods, worms, mollusks, and many other groups.

Vertebrates and most invertebrates have a head, where sense organs are concentrated and legs, wings, or fins for locomotion. Vertebrates and many invertebrates, such as the arthropods and worms, have bilateral, or two-sided, symmetry. This means that they have two mirror-image sides (a right side and a left side), distinct upper and lower surfaces of the body, and a distinct front and rear.

Some invertebrates, such as jellyfish, sea anemones, and sea stars, or starfish, display radial symmetry, similar to that of a wheel, in which the parts of the body are arranged around a central axis. Animals with radial symmetry live in marine or freshwa ter aquatic environments. Some drift with the currents, unable to swim in any definite direction. Others become attached to a solid object by one end and float with the mouth end upright. Tentacles arranged in a circle around the mouth sweep in food particles and ward off enemies.

## HOW INVERTEBRATES MOVE

Mollusks have soft bodies that are in most species enclosed in hard, hinged shells. Snails

have a single large, fleshy foot that can extend outside its shell. Oysters, clams, mussels, and scallops also have a single muscular foot that they use to burrow into sand. These mollusks do not move around efficiently. Oysters fasten themselves to something solid and settle down for life, letting food drift to them. Scallops may move in a zigzag motion by clapping their shells together. The octopus and

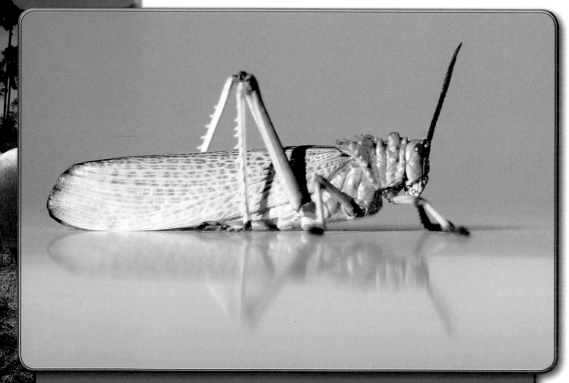

*A grasshopper rests on a car roof in South Africa.* **Paul Ellis/AFP/ Getty Images**

the squid have a head that is surrounded by a circle of eight or ten tentacles, respectively, that act as arms and feet. They use jets of water to propel themselves through the water.

Joint-legged animals, or arthropods, have bodies divided into segments that have specialized functions. These animals also have many jointed legs. Most arthropods are covered with a jointed skeleton made of a horny material. This outside skeleton is lighter than the shells of the mollusks. The legs and muscles and many organs of the arthropod are attached to the outside skeleton.

The arthropods include insects, such as houseflies and ladybugs; crustaceans, such as lobsters, crabs, and copepods; arachnids, such as spiders, scorpions, and ticks; and other organisms, such as centipedes and millipedes. Arthropods can run, jump, swim, and crawl. Some live mostly on land, while others live mostly in water. Many of the insects have wings and can fly.

## HOW BACKBONED ANIMALS MOVE

Many vertebrates can move through water and air or over the ground with great speed and skill. Birds, with their feathered wings, are the best fliers. Fish are the best swimmers. However, other vertebrates also can fly and swim. Bats fly on wings made of a skinlike membrane. The flying squirrel glides by using a broad membrane that lies between its legs, and the flying fish can

*A kangaroo shows its ability to jump as it flees a bushfire in Australia's Kiewa Valley on February 11, 2009.* **Torsten Blackwood/ AFP/Getty Images**

soar over the surface of the ocean by using its fins; however, neither can move very far through the air.

A number of mammals are good swimmers, including whales, which spend their entire life in the ocean, and seals, which also spend time on land. Some turtles swim with paddlelike front legs, and some water birds can swim underwater with their wings. The mudskipper and walking catfish are fish that can walk on mud by pulling themselves along on their front fins.

Frogs, kangaroos, and various cats are superior jumpers. Some fish are also able to jump. Salmon leap up waterfalls when they travel from the sea to their home streams to lay their eggs. Tarpon, swordfish, and sailfish make great leaps out of the water when pursuing their prey or trying to escape an enemy.

## BREATHING

All animals must take in oxygen in order to change food into a form that the body can use. Some animals that live in water absorb oxygen directly into their cells. The sponge, a very simple animal, is a good example. The

surface of a sponge is covered with millions of tiny pores. Water that bears dissolved oxygen and minute food particles flows in through the pores and is discharged from an opening at the top of the sponge.

Fish and tadpoles (amphibian larvae) breathe by means of gills. Caterpillars and adult insects take air into the body through breathing pores called spiracles.

Mammals, birds, and reptiles obtain oxygen from the air. They take air into the lungs, and the oxygen passes into red blood cells through membranes in the lungs. The bloodstream then carries the oxygen to all parts of the body. Adult amphibians have lungs, but they also have thin, moist skins that absorb oxygen directly.

## REPRODUCTION

All animals can reproduce, creating offspring of their own kind. Some simple animals reproduce asexually, in which a mating partner is not needed. Sea squirts, for example, reproduce by budding: lumps appear along a branchlike organ and develop into young sea squirts. Sea squirts, sponges, corals, and other organisms that bud often remain together and form large colonies.

# REPRODUCTIVE FACTS OF COMMON MAMMALS

| ANIMAL | AGE AT WHICH FEMALE IS SEXUALLY MATURE | GESTA-TION PERIOD, IN DAYS | AVERAGE NUMBER OF OFFSPRING PER LITTER | AVERAGE WEIGHT OF OFFSPRING AT BIRTH (METRIC) |
|---|---|---|---|---|
| armadillo | 1 year | 150 | 1–12 | 3 ounces (85 grams) |
| bear, black | 4–5 years | 210–220 | 2–3 | 11 ounces (300 grams) |
| bear, polar | 5 years | 240 | 1–4 | 20 ounces (600 grams) |
| cat, domestic | 7–12 months | 65 | 1–8 | 3 ounces (100 grams) |
| cattle | 18 months | 280–290 | 1 | 50 pounds (23 kilograms) |
| chimpanzee | 7 years | 230 | 1 | 4 pounds (2 kilograms) |
| dog | 10–24 months | 59–69 | 3–10 | 8 ounces (230 grams) |
| donkey | 2–3 years | 365–380 | 1 | 50 pounds (23 kilograms) |
| elephant, African | 14 years | 645 | 1 | 243 pounds (110 kilograms) |
| elephant, Indian | 9–12 years | 645 | 1 | 220 pounds (100 kilograms) |
| giraffe | 3½ years | 450 | 1 | 132 pounds (60 kilograms) |
| guinea pig | 2–3 months | 68 | 1–13 | 4 ounces (100 grams) |
| horse | 2–3 years | 337 | 1 | 50 pounds (23 kilograms) |
| kangaroo | 20–36 months | 40–45* | 1 | 0.03 ounce (0.85 gram) |
| lion | 3–4 years | 108 | 1–6 | 3 pounds (1.4 kilograms) |
| mole | 10 months | 30 | 2–5 | 0.04 ounce (1 gram) |
| mouse, house | 5–7 weeks | 20–21 | 3–12 | 0.04 ounce (1 gram) |
| opossum | 275 days | 13* | 7–9 | 0.004 ounce (0.1 gram) |
| rabbit | 80 days | 30–32 | 2–15 | 2 ounces (57 grams) |
| whale, humpback | 6–12 years | 334–365 | 1 | 3,000 pounds (1,350 kilograms) |

*Marsupial. Figure does not include extended stay in maternal pouch.

The hydra also reproduces by budding, but in time the young bud separates and goes off to grow and live alone.

In sexual reproduction, a male and a female organism each contribute toward creating offspring. Most animals reproduce by means of eggs from the female that are fertilized by sperm from the male.

The fertilized eggs of some species are deposited in a nest or in some other manner before hatching. Most species of mammal and some species of reptile and fish bear their young alive—the fertilized eggs develop within the body of the female.

The types of reproductive behavior among animals are almost as varied as the kinds of animals themselves. Some species, such as most insects and turtles, deposit their eggs and give them no further attention. In contrast, social insects, such as ants and bees, form colonies in which a single female lays all of the eggs, and workers provide care and nourishment for the developing young in the nest. The females of some reptiles, such as the king cobra and the blue-tailed skink, and amphibians, such as the marble salamander, stay with their clutch of eggs until they hatch but

*Two German cockroaches mate end-to-end.* **Bates Littlehales/National Geographic Image Collection/Getty Images**

provide no protection or nourishment for the young. Some fish guard their young after they are born. Crocodilians protect the eggs before hatching and the young for several months afterwards. Many birds provide not only protection but also nourishment for the developing young. Mammals, which

feed their young with milk produced by the mother, provide care for their young much longer than do other animals.

## HOMES

Many animals build temporary or permanent homes for themselves and their young. Birds occupy their nests only while they are incubating eggs and feeding the helpless nestlings. A few fish make temporary nests for their young.

One notable animal dwelling is the water-protected lodge that beavers build. Almost as remarkable is the dome-shaped winter home of the muskrat. Underground burrows with sleeping rooms, food-storage rooms, connecting tunnels, and emergency exits are constructed by groundhogs, prairie dogs, European rabbits, gophers, kangaroo rats, and field mice. Chimpanzees and gorillas build temporary nests and sleeping platforms of sticks in trees. The living quarters made by the different kinds of ants can be intricate and complex. Certain tropical bats cut palm fronds in such a way that they droop to form a leafy shelter from the hot sun and torrential rains.

## DEFENSES

All animals have some means of defending themselves against enemies. A cat can usually outrun a dog and climb the nearest tree. If cornered, it will scratch and bite.

Many animals rely on speed, camouflage, teeth, claws, and even intimidation to escape other animals. The variety of means of protection is extensive. Porcupines and hedgehogs roll into a ball and raise their sharp quills.

A young Père David's deer, born at Knowsley Safari Park in Merseyside, England, shows the spots that keep it camouflaged in woodland settings. AFP/Getty Images

# BEAVERS, MASTER ENGINEERS

A mammal belonging to the order of rodents, or gnawing animals, the beaver has been recognized as a master engineer. Beavers live in a structure called a lodge. By using their teeth and paws, beavers construct a lodge in a riverbank or in a pond created by a dam. From a distance, a beaver lodge resembles a heap of tree branches and mud. It consists of a platform of carefully interlaced branches held together by clay and dead leaves. When the platform has been built up a few inches above the water, the beavers fashion a dome-shaped roof over it.

Entrances to the beaver lodge often open underwater, so that the animals may pass in and out below the winter ice. There are at least two, and up to five, such entrances. A steep and narrow entrance is used by the beavers for entry and exit. Another entrance is used for the transportation of wood for winter food. These underwater entrances help protect the beavers from attacks by predators.

*A beaver lodge is depicted with one side cut away in order to show how it is built. The floor has two levels as a protection in case the water rises during a spring thaw. Entrances are built to be below the ice that may cover the pond in winter. A store of wood is kept outside the underwater doorway. Fresh air filters through the walls, but there may be an air hole in the top.* **Encyclopædia Britannica, Inc.**

The quills come off and stick into the nose or paw of an unwary dog or some other enemy. Skunks spray a foul-smelling fluid from a gland when they are frightened. Deer, moose, and antelope fight with their antlers. Squids shoot out a cloud of inky material and escape under its cover. The electric ray and several other kinds of fish have built-in electric storage cells by which they can deliver a paralyzing shock. Some insects, snakes, and lizards protect themselves with their venom. Many amphibians produce poisonous skin secretions.

Many animals hide by means of protective coloration. A baby deer is almost invisible in the forest because its spotted coat looks like patches of sunlight in the brown leaves. Many fish, birds, insects, lizards, and snakes use nature's camouflage to avoid being seen.

## FEEDING

Animals display a wide diversity in feeding behaviors and strategies. The hydra feeds most commonly on the larvae of a kind of shellfish. It has a mouth surrounded by long tentacles. The tentacles sting and paralyze the prey and then shove it inside the mouth.

*A great mormon butterfly drinks nectar from a flower in Hong Kong, China.* **AFP/Getty Images**

Butterflies and moths have tubelike mouth parts. With these they suck nectar from flowers. Grasshoppers and beetles have chewing, grasping, and tearing mouthparts.

Bats and many kinds of birds catch insects in flight. Some birds comb leaves with their bills for small insects, and woodpeckers

29

hammer into the bark of trees for grubs. Hawks swoop down to hunt rodents and other birds.

The kangaroo rat feeds on dry thistle and cactus leaves, seeds, and small juicy tubers that grow below the surface. It collects seeds in its cheek pouches and stores them in underground chambers. Gophers and chipmunks also collect food in their cheek pouches and store it in underground pantries for future use.

## CARNIVORES AND HERBIVORES

Animals that eat other animals are called carnivores. The shark is a fierce carnivore. It lives on smaller fish, such as mackerel. Many mammals are carnivores. Carnivorous animals have special kinds of teeth for tearing their food into chunks and chewing it. Most of them have claws for catching and holding their prey. Among the carnivores are cats, dogs, raccoons, weasels, bears, hyenas, and civet cats.

The blue whale, despite its great size, eats krill, shrimplike creatures only about 1 inch (2.5 centimeters) in length. When it finds a school of krill, it opens its mouth and gulps in several barrelfuls of water. Baleen—horny bristles that hang from the roof of its mouth—strains the krill from the water.

Animals that feed on insects are known as insectivores. A few mammals are insectivores, including moles, shrews, hedgehogs, bats, armadillos, aardvarks, and anteaters.

*A cheetah carries a live impala fawn to train her two cubs in the art of chasing in Masai-Mara game reserve in Kenya.* **Mladen Antonov/ AFP/Getty Images**

Many bird species are also insect eaters, as are certain kinds of insects, such as ladybugs.

A large group of animals are herbivores, which means they eat producer organisms, namely plants and algae. Many herbivores are prey of the carnivores. Insects are the dominant herbivores in most parts of the world, though they may be less conspicuous than plant-eating mammals and birds. Herbivorous mammals include horses, cattle, sheep, goats, rabbits, rodents, deer and antelope, and elephants.

Animals that eat both animal and plant matter are referred to as omnivores. Omnivores include bears as well as many small mammals and birds.

# CHAPTER 2

# CLASSIFICATION AND BEHAVIOR

Determining how animals evolved and how they should be classified are two important matters for biologists who study animal life. Another fascinating area of inquiry is the amazingly varied behavior of animals. The study of animal behavior has, in fact, become a scientific specialty, practiced by researchers who try to find out why animals act in the specific ways they do—for

*Elephants walk with their calves in the Serengeti National Park in northern Tanzania.* Tony Karumba/AFP/Getty Images

instance, why some animals migrate or live together in groups—and how their behavior helps them and their offspring survive.

## BEGINNINGS OF ANIMAL LIFE

Scientists think that the first organisms in the history of the Earth were simple single-celled organisms that arose around 3.5 billion years ago, roughly a billion years after the Earth was formed. These early organisms may have lived in warm, salty pools containing carbon, nitrogen, oxygen, and hydrogen. Later organisms developed from having one cell to having many cells, becoming more and more complex. As the environment changed over many millions of years, these early organisms underwent a process known as natural selection, giving rise in time to the first animals that lived in the oceans. Eventually, some animals moved into freshwater. Others began to live on land. Over time, the Earth underwent geologic and atmospheric changes, which caused some kinds of animals to die out and others to adapt to the changed environment and thrive. The changes resulted in the great diversity of animal life we see today.

Exactly when and how animals evolved from the earliest simple forms to the diversity

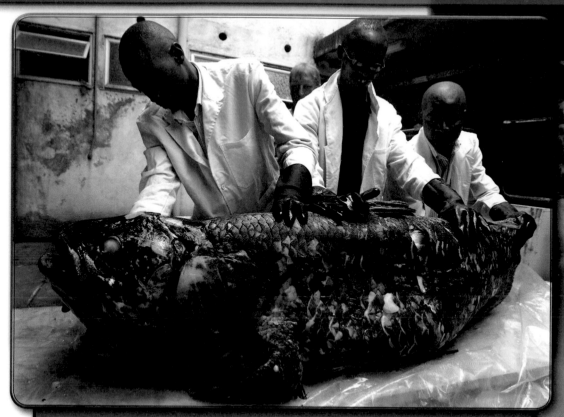

*Members of the National Museum of Kenya show a 170 lb. (77 kgs.) coelacanth caught by Kenyan fishermen. This ancient type of fish was thought to have vanished with the dinosaurs.* Simon Maina/AFP/ Getty Images

that exists today are questions that continue to challenge biologists. Many different hypotheses have been presented as new evidence is uncovered and studied. What is clear is that at some point hundreds of millions of years after the earliest animals evolved, a group of animals called chordates arose that had the

35

beginnings of an internal skeleton and a rudimentary backbone in the form of a notochord, a semiflexible structure made of cartilage. In addition to their rudimentary backbones, the early chordates also had a cord of nervous tissue running along their backs—the forerunner of a spinal cord. Within this group arose a subgroup of animals with an internal skeleton and spine made of bone. This latter group included the earliest vertebrates. Today, vertebrates are among the most familiar animals, although they make up only about 5 percent of all animal species. They include mammals, reptiles, birds, fish, and amphibians. Invertebrates—animals without backbones—make up the remaining 95 percent of animal species. Invertebrates include sponges, corals, jellyfish, clams, lobsters, starfish, and insects.

More than 1 million insect species have been described, though scientists believe that represents far less than the total number. Still, this makes insects the largest group within the animal kingdom. In comparison, there are only some 5,000 species of mammals.

## How Animals Are Classified

To study the many forms of animal life in a systematic way, scientists have divided the animal kingdom into groups. These groups are largely based upon the structure of the animal's body. The largest divisions are phyla (singular, phylum). The word phylum means "race" or "tribe." The phyla are groups of animals with fundamentally different body plans.

Each phylum is divided into classes, the classes into orders, and the orders into families. Families are subdivided into genera (singular, genus), and each genus is divided into species. All members of the same species are closely related. They are capable of interbreeding and producing fertile offspring. Animals of different species normally do not interbreed. Every animal has a binomial scientific name—that is, a name consisting of two parts, the genus and species.

## HOW CLASSIFICATION SHOWS RELATIONSHIPS

The classification of animals shows different levels of relationships, from remotely related members of the same phylum to closely related species within a genus. House cats (Felis catus) and sand cats (Felis margarita) belong to the same genus (Felis) and family (Felidae) but to different species.

Dogs and cats do not appear to be related. Both, however, have backbones and are meat-eating mammals. Hence they belong to phylum Chordata (having a spinal cord), class Mammalia (mammals), and order Carnivora (flesh eaters); because of differences between them, however, they belong to separate families (dog, Canidae; cat, Felidae).

Whales and sharks both appear to be kinds of fish. Both are strong, streamlined

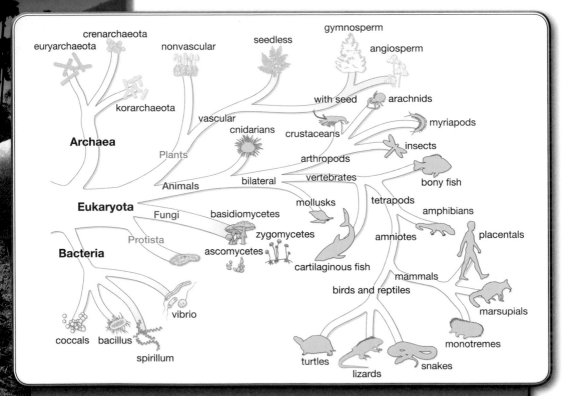

*The tree of life according to the three-domain system.* **Encyclopædia Britannica, Inc.**

swimmers of the sea. However, the whale is a mammal. It has lungs and is warm-blooded, gives birth to live young, and nurses its offspring with milk. Whales therefore belong to the class Mammalia. The shark, on the other hand, is a primitive kind of fish with a skeleton of cartilage instead of bone. Sharks, whales, and true fish all have a backbone. Thus, they are placed in the same phylum

*A giant schnauzer and a cat check each other out in Leipzig, Germany.*
**Peter Endig/AFP/Getty Images**

(Chordata) and subphylum (Vertebrata). Sharks and bony fish, however, are also in different subgroups, the sharks being in the class Chondrichthyes and the bony fish in the superclass Osteichthyes.

Classification also suggests which kinds of animals may have descended (evolved) from other types. All multicellular animals, for example, are believed to be descendants of single-celled animals. This does not mean descent from one kind of animal living today to another, however. All living animals are believed to have descended from common ancestors that were less specialized. These relationships may be shown on a treelike diagram called a phylogenetic tree. The word phylogenetic comes from two Greek words meaning "race history."

## *ANIMALS AND THEIR SENSES*

All animals have the ability to sense and respond to their surroundings. The more highly developed animals have sense organs to perceive light, sound, touch, taste, and smell.

Eyes are very important to most mammals. Animals that hunt and feed by night have very large eyes. The eyes of cats and some nocturnal animals have pupils that can open wide in the dark and narrow down to slits in the sunlight. Insects have compound eyes, made up of tiny units that break up the image into many small images. They also have two or three simple eyes that probably detect motion. The eyesight of some fish is especially keen.

Ears are perhaps as important as eyes to some species. The fennec is a foxlike animal that lives in the Sahara and hunts by night. Its large ears help it detect its prey in the darkness of a hot, dry climate, where food may be very scarce.

The cat is also a night prowler, and it too has large, erect ears. The hearing organs of the field cricket and katydid are located on their forelegs; the organ is a thin membrane that vibrates in response to sound waves.

Many animals have sense organs that are different from those of mammals. The antennae of moths, butterflies, and other insects are the organs of taste, touch, smell, and hearing.

The barbels of the catfish and the whiskers of the flying squirrel and the domestic cat are organs of touch. They are very useful for animals that explore in the dark. The lateral line of the fish is a rod of nerve cells running the length of the body. It probably helps fish sense movements in the surrounding water.

*Fennecs, like these shown at the Cabosse animal park in Jurques, France, are noted for their large ears.* **Mychele Daniau/AFP/Getty Images**

The delicate forked tongue of the snake tastes the air. With it the snake can locate food and other snakes. The rattlesnake has sensory pits on the head that can detect the infrared radiation, or heat, from nearby animals, enabling it to locate potential prey in the dark. Even the simplest animals respond to touch. If a flatworm is touched, it may jerk away or curl up into a ball. It moves away from strong light or from water that is too hot or too cold.

In the warm, muddy rivers of western Africa there are fish that send out small electric impulses and surround themselves with an electric field. The fish are made aware of the approach of other organisms by changes in the electric field. This system therefore takes the place of eyesight in the dark waters and keeps the fish informed of their surroundings. Bats emit high-pitched squeaks and use the reflected sound waves to avoid objects and locate prey while flying. Dolphins and whales send out ultrasonic signals and are able to detect objects by reflections of the sound.

## *MIGRATION AND HIBERNATION*

When winter comes to northern or high-mountain regions, many birds and some mammals seek a milder climate by moving to

a different region or to a lower elevation. They are said to migrate. Other kinds of mammals (bears and woodchucks, for example) store up fat in their bodies in the fall by eating as much food as they can. Then they curl up in a cave or some other protected place and enter into a sleeplike state of reduced energy consumption called hibernation.

Most insects die in the wintertime. They leave well-protected eggs that hatch in the spring. Fish, frogs, and aquatic arthropods and other water-dwelling animals may hibernate in mud or move to deeper water and become inactive.

Many species of animals, including mammals, fish, birds, and insects, migrate to specific areas to breed. A notable example is the migration of Pacific salmon, which leave the ocean and swim up fast-flowing rivers to freshwater spawning areas.

## LIVING TOGETHER IN GROUPS

Some animals live with others of their own kind. Ants, honeybees and bumblebees, and wasps are called social insects because they live together in highly organized societies.

Some birds live in large colonies. Penguins, anis, and eider ducks are examples. Weaver

*Wildebeest cross the Mara River during their annual migration through the Massai Mara National Reserve in western Kenya in 2008.* Roberto Schmidt/ AFP/Getty Images

finches work together to build huge community dwellings.

Some large herbivorous mammals such as gazelles, wildebeest, and elephants live together in herds. This behavior helps provide protection against predators. Baboons live in groups called troops, and they cooperate in getting food and post sentries to watch for danger. South American monkeys travel through forests in family groups. They may scatter while they are searching for food, but stay within sight or hearing of one another.

*A bee drinks nectar from a flower in Hohen Neuendorf, Germany.*
**Michael Urban/AFP/Getty Images**

## RELATIONSHIP TO HUMANS

Humans rely on other animals in a variety of ways. For example, the domestication of animals has been important to the development of civilization. By pollinating flowers, bees help in the cultivation of orchard fruits, alfalfa, clover, and many vegetables. The earthworm, by churning up the soil, improves the growth of plants.

Birds eat insect pests, weed seeds, and rodents. Certain bats eat so many mosquitoes and other insects that some communities have erected shelters for bats to encourage them to stay in the area. Hyenas, vultures, and carrion beetles keep regions clean by devouring dead animals.

Countless animal products are used by humans: pearls (from the oyster), shellac and lacquer (from the lac insect), glue, and fertilizers are only a few examples. Important drugs are produced from the blood and glands of certain animals. Horses and other animals serve as hosts for producing antivenins for snakebite that are obtained from their blood. Experiments performed on such animals as rats, mice, guinea pigs, and monkeys have been responsible for important advances in medical knowledge and the conquest of human disease.

# How Animals Became Domesticated

Cattle, sheep, pigs, goats, and horses—the most important and widespread of the domestic animals—are all hoofed grass eaters and can be kept in herds. All of them were first mastered by the early peoples of southwestern Asia. It has been suggested that the grassy plains of that region began slowly eroding some 10,000 years ago. Humans were forced to share smaller and smaller oases of fertile land with wild animals. People gradually learned how to control the animals. Some animals were bred in

*Sheep stand in a snow-covered field on December 25, 2010, in Letterkenny, Ireland.* Gareth Cattermole/Getty Images

captivity, and from them the domestic strains developed.

Another theory of how domestication came about points to the widespread human practice of making pets of captured young and crippled animals. Certain kinds of creatures became attached to their human masters. They followed the camps, and slowly humans built up herds. Several factors, rather than any one simple cause, must have led to domestication.

Some animals are harmful to humans. Insect pests cause billions of dollars' worth of damage every year. Animal parasites can cause serious diseases of the human body and of domesticated animals. Fleas and mosquitoes are carriers of microorganisms that cause such serious conditions as malaria and encephalitis.

# CHAPTER 3

# ANIMALS WITHOUT BACKBONES

All members of the animal kingdom (Animalia) are multicellular—that is, all have bodies composed of many cells. Multicellular animals are sometimes referred to as metazoans, to distinguish them from the protozoans—single-celled organisms that once were classified as animals and later grouped in the kingdom Protista. The simplest animals make up the phylum Porifera ("pore bearers"). The most familiar kinds are the sponges. They are called pore bearers because they are covered with millions of tiny pores, or openings. Sponges take in oxygen and the tiny waterborne organisms that constitute their food from the water that flows into the pores and then eject water that contains wastes through a separate, larger opening. Sponges have no mouth or digestive cavity, no nervous system, and no circulatory system. Several types of cells are present, but unlike the cells in more complex animals, each generally functions as a unit without forming tissues, as in more complex metazoans. (Tissues are groups of similar cells bound together to perform a common function.)

# ANIMALS IN THE SHAPE OF A POUCH

The next, least complex structural pattern in invertebrates is that of a hollow gut. The representative phylum is Cnidaria, a term stemming from the Greek word koilos (hollow). Among the cnidarians are the corals, hydras, jellyfishes, and sea anemones. The body is composed of two tissue layers. The inner layer, or endoderm, lines the central digestive cavity. The outer layer, or ectoderm, protects the animal externally.

The cnidarians have a mouthlike opening—the only opening into the gut—that takes in food and ejects waste material. Food-gathering organs such as tentacles and

*Sponges, flatworms, jellyfish, starfish, spiders, shrimp, snails, and scallops are just a few of the many kinds of invertebrates.* **Encyclopædia Britannica, Inc.**

Invertebrates

flatworm

sponge

jellyfish

starfish

snail

scallop

spider

shrimp

protective structures such as stinging cells surround the mouth. There is a rudimentary nervous system. Cnidarians are headless creatures with radial symmetry; they have similar body parts arranged around a central axis. Some drift around in ocean currents, unable to swim efficiently in any particular direction. Some of them in their adult stages—the corals, for example—fasten themselves to fixed objects.

## FLATWORMS

Flatworms called planaria are interesting because they are the simplest kind of animal that has a definite head and bilateral symmetry. Planaria belong to the phylum Platyhelminthes (flatworms). The mouth is on the underside of the triangular head, which bears sense organs.

Platyhelminthes are also the simplest living animals to have three tissue layers. Between the ectoderm and the endoderm, which first appeared in the jellyfish and their relatives, is a middle layer: the mesoderm. Animals without a mesoderm are small and fragile. This third layer gives solidity to the body and permits the animal to grow to a large size. Muscles and other complex organs develop from this layer.

# ROUNDWORMS

Roundworms, unlike flatworms, have a digestive tube with two openings—a mouth and an anus through which wastes are expelled. Roundworms, which make up the phylum Nematoda, are also called nematodes. Roundworms are among the most abundant of all animals and are found in a wide variety of environments. Parasitic roundworms are responsible for a number of diseases in humans, including trichinosis and hookworm disease.

*Nematodes like these roundworms are the most numerous of larger decomposers in compost.* **Bianca Lavies/ National Geographic Image Collection/ Getty Images**

## SEGMENTED WORMS

Segmented worms, like roundworms, have a digestive tube with a mouth and an anus. The phylum Annelida (meaning ringed, or segmented) has a digestive system built on the same plan as the vertebrates. Unlike roundworms, the digestive tube of segmented worms is lined by a mesodermal tissue layer. Earthworms and leeches are familiar annelids.

## THE SOFT-BODIED ANIMALS

The phylum Mollusca (from the Latin word for "soft") includes the clam, oyster, chiton, snail, octopus, and squid. Mollusks have soft, fleshy bodies not divided into segments. The main part of the body is enclosed in a fold of tissue called the mantle. They have bilateral symmetry. Many kinds of mollusks are covered by a shell.

## ARTHROPODS: THE LARGEST GROUP OF ANIMALS

The phylum Arthropoda ("jointed foot") has the largest number of species. In fact, about 85 percent of known species are arthropods, and insects alone make up about 75 percent of known species.

Other arthropods include the centipedes and millipedes; the arachnids (spiders, scorpions, ticks, mites); and the crustaceans (barnacles, crabs, crayfish, lobsters, shrimp, water fleas). Obviously, the arthropod body plan has been highly successful. The members of this phylum live on land, in fresh

*People look at a plastic box full of Madagascar hissing cockroaches in Bangkok, Thailand. Like other insects, cockroaches' exoskeletons are made of chitin.* **Pornchai Kittiwongsakul/AFP/Getty Images**

water, and in salt water. They can walk, fly, burrow, and swim. This is the only invertebrate group with jointed appendages (legs, feet, and antennae).

Arthropods, like mollusks, wear a supporting framework, or exoskeleton, on the outside of the body. Much more highly developed than the heavy, clumsy shell of the clams and snails, it is made of a substance called chitin. Rigid, waterproof plates of chitin are joined by thin, flexible membranes of chitin so that the animal can move freely and quickly. The muscles are attached to the inner surface of the armor. Many important structures are connected to the outer surface. For example, the wings, legs, jaws, and antennae of the insects are all made of chitin and are attached to the outer skeleton. The body is divided into sections, or segments.

## *Spiny-Skinned Animals*

One phylum with the characteristics of several others is the Echinodermata ("spiny-skinned"). All members of the group, which includes sea stars (commonly called starfish), sea urchins, sea cucumbers, and sea lilies, live in salt water—some in the shallow shoreline waters, others in the ocean depths.

# THE SOCIABLE—AND WARLIKE—ANT

The most distinguishing trait of ant behavior is sociability. Ants do not act individually; they behave according to the needs of the colony in roles dictated by the caste into which they are born. The major social unit is the colony, which forms a nest.

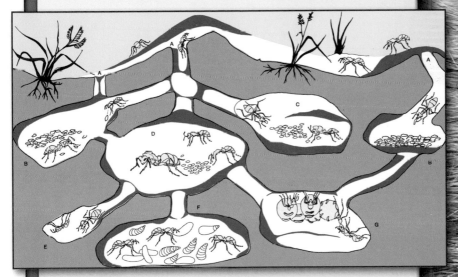

*An ant colony has several entrances (A), leading to a variety of subterranean chambers. Each chamber has a specific use. Some are for food storage (B). The queen has her own room (D). In another chamber workers tend unhatched eggs (C). A deeper room serves as a nursery for larvae and cocoons (F). In the replete gallery (G) are the worker ants whose expanded abdomens contain surplus food for the colony. In another room (E), worker ants are digging a new chamber.* Encyclopædia Britannica, Inc.

Most of an ant's life is spent in its nest with from a few to more than a million other individuals. Some ants dig chambers and passages in the ground; others locate their nests under rocks, in trees, or in logs.

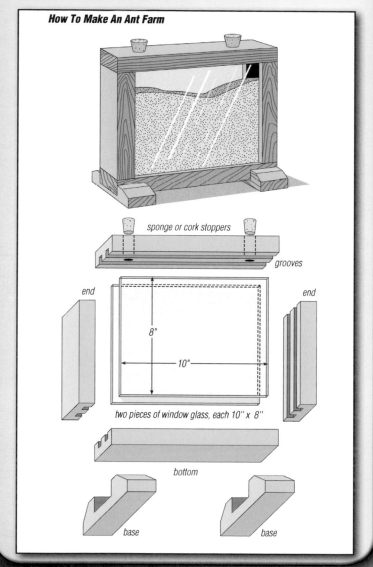

**How To Make An Ant Farm**

sponge or cork stoppers

grooves

end

end

8"

10"

two pieces of window glass, each 10" x 8"

bottom

base

base

The social structure of the colony has led to several unusual living arrangements. Ants can be very hospitable. Some species live as guests with other ants or insects; some ants host other insects as guests. A few species live with parasites—insects or other small animals, such as mites, spiders, caterpillars, and beetles, that are fed and sheltered by the colony but that provide nothing in return.

Hospitality and cooperation are only one aspect of the ant's social character, however. It is also capable of warlike behavior. Ants are the only animals other than humans that carry on organized warfare, usually for the capture of slaves.

The dependence on slaves is clearly evident in the amazon ants. Because of physical limitations, they are inefficient workers. They use other species in their colony to care for their young, expand the nest, and do the other chores of the worker caste. The ant's aggressive nature is also seen in robberies and quarrels over boundaries, which can lead to feuds lasting for years between different colonies of ants.

*A simple ant farm can be made from two pieces of glass fitted into four sections of grooved wood and set on a wooden base. Fill the assembled farm two-thirds full with soil found near an anthill. A colony must contain a queen and should also have eggs, larvae, pupae, and parasites, along with the other ants. Ants should be fed bits of ground beef, dead insects, bread crumbs, and watered honey. The cork or sponge stoppers should be kept moist; ants must have moisture.* **Encyclopædia Britannica, Inc.**

The young, called larvae, have bilateral symmetry, but the adults have radial symmetry, like the cnidaria. The Echinodermata have an endoskeleton, or skeleton that is embedded in the flesh. It consists of a meshwork of plates that are made of calcium. The plates are joined by connective tissue and muscles. Spines project from these plates.

# CHAPTER 4

# ANIMALS WITH BACKBONES

The most complex members of the animal kingdom belong to the phylum Chordata. Most members of this phylum are vertebrates—that is, they have a backbone. Groups of primitive chordates known as tunicates and cephalochordates, however, do not have a backbone.

The major subdivisions of the vertebrates are the fish, amphibians, reptiles, birds, and mammals. Members of this phylum possess the following structures at some period of their life, either as embryos or as adults: a notochord, a nerve tube, and pharyngeal gill slits or pouches.

A notochord is an internal supporting rod extending the length of the body. It is found in the embryos of all chordates, including human beings. Only the most primitive chordates, such as the amphioxus, or lancelet, the lamprey, and the hagfish, retain the notochord as adults, though remnants of the notochord are also present in sharks. In other chordates, such as amphibians, reptiles, birds, and mammals, the notochord is replaced during development of the embryo

## Vertebrates

fishes

amphibians

reptiles

birds

mammals

whale

groundhog

human

**The major groups of vertebrates include fish, amphibians, reptiles, birds, and mammals.** Encyclopædia Britannica, Inc.

by a bony column of vertebrae, which gives the column and the animal flexibility.

The nerve tube structure lies in the midline of the body on the top (dorsal side) of the notochord. In the annelid worms and the arthropods, in contrast, the main nerve is solid and lies on the underside (ventral side). In most chordates the forward end of the nerve tube forms a brain; the remainder is the spinal cord.

Some chordates, such as fish, breathe through openings in the side of the neck in the region of the pharynx. These openings are known as pharyngeal gill slits. The embryos of more complex chordates have pouch-like openings instead of slits, but they disappear in the adult.

## PRIMITIVE CHORDATES

The small marine animal known as the amphioxus is one of the nonvertebrate chordates. This animal is a slender, semi-transparent sea dweller about 4 inches (10 centimeters) long. Scientists believe that it may be closely related to the common ancestor of the vertebrates. The amphioxus has a

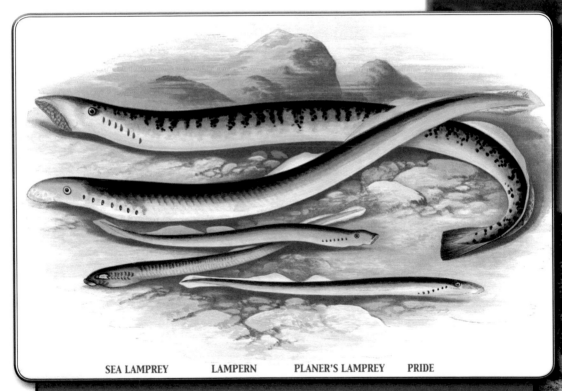

SEA LAMPREY    LAMPERN    PLANER'S LAMPREY    PRIDE

*Assorted lampreys.* **Buyenlarge/Archive Photos/Getty Images**

notochord and a tubular nerve cord along the back. It does not have a well-developed brain, however, and has only traces of eyes and ears. Pigment spots along the body are sensitive to light. The pharyngeal gill slits strain food from the water. The tunicates, or sea squirts, and acorn worms are other primitive chordates.

Lampreys are among the simplest true vertebrates. They have a notochord. The skeleton is composed of cartilage. They lack jaws and paired limbs.

## FISH

Many animals that live in water are called fish. Perch, crayfish, cuttlefish, jellyfish, and even whales and dolphins all live in water. Yet, of these animals, only the perch is a true fish. Whales and dolphins are warm-blooded mammals. The others belong to the great group of animals without backbones, called invertebrates.

A fish is a cold-blooded animal that has a backbone and lives in water and breathes by means of gills. It normally has two pairs of fins in place of arms and legs, as well as several other fins. Many fish are covered with scales.

Certain other animals live in water at least part of the time. They too have backbones, and early in their lives they breathe underwater by means of gills. These are the amphibians—primarily frogs, toads, and salamanders. How, then, can one tell fish from amphibians? Among the differences are that fish have fins as appendages and most fish have scales that cover the body. Most adult amphibians have legs and no body scales. Fish never have true legs.

## *AMPHIBIANS*

Four hundred million years ago, the most advanced forms of life on Earth, the fish, lived in the water. Plants and insects alone occupied the land until the appearance of the amphibians more than 350 million years ago. Almost all amphibians have features that fall between those of fish and those of reptiles. The most commonly known amphibians are frogs, toads, and salamanders. Although most have changed very little since they first began to breathe on land, some of the early amphibians were the ancestors of today's reptiles, birds, and mammals.

*Frogs, like this colorful poisonous frog, are amphibians who spend their lives both in fresh water and on land.* **Yuri Cortez/AFP/Getty Images**

The word amphibian comes from the Greek *amphi*, meaning "both," and *bios*, meaning "life." It describes cold-blooded animals with backbones that pass their lives both in fresh water and on land. Because amphibians live in water and on land, their natural environments are shores, ponds, marshes, swamps, and low-lying meadows.

## REPTILES

According to fossil records, reptiles first appeared on Earth more than 300 million years ago. In fact, birds and mammals evolved from reptilian ancestors. Reptiles are distinguished from other vertebrates by the fact that they have dry scales covering their

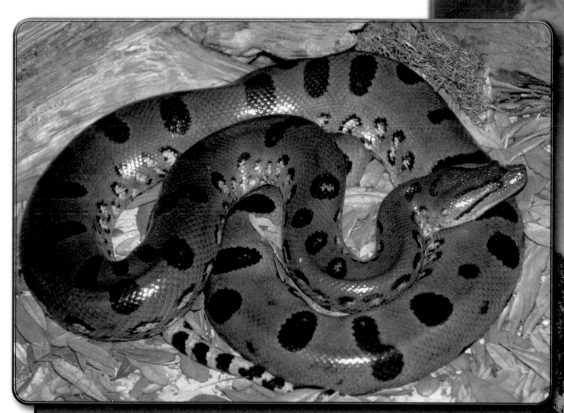

*Giant anaconda* **(Eunectes murinus).** © **Z. Leszczynski/Animals Animals**

bodies. Reptiles are further distinguished from vertebrates lower on the evolutionary scale by their ability to perform internal fertilization, whereby the male places sperm inside the female. The scales of reptiles differ in structure and development from those of fish, and, unlike amphibians, reptiles have few or no glands present in their skin. Unlike birds and mammals, which maintain relatively constant internal temperatures, the body temperature of reptiles is directly

*Ichthyosaur (Ichthyosaurus species).* **Encyclopædia Britannica, Inc.**

affected by the temperature of the reptiles' surroundings. The brains of reptiles are proportionally much smaller than those of similar-sized mammals.

Reptiles produce amniotic eggs, which differ from those of amphibians by having special membranes and a shell that help prevent the embryo from drying up in a terrestrial environment where moisture levels may be low. It was due largely to their amniotic eggs that reptiles became the first vertebrates to adapt completely to life on land.

Among the reptiles are present-day snakes, lizards, turtles, crocodiles, and alligators, as well as thousands of extinct species. Earlier reptiles included ichthyosaurs and pterosaurs. The tuatara of New Zealand is the sole living member of its taxonomic order.

## BIRDS

Just exactly what is a bird? Perhaps you would say that a bird is an animal that flies. But butterflies, which are insects, and bats, which are mammals, also fly. Some birds, on the other hand, do not fly at all. The ostrich, the emu, and the kiwi run very fast.

69

*Ostriches at an ostrich farm near Tyre, Lebanon.* **AFP/Getty Images**

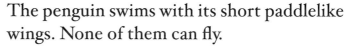

The penguin swims with its short paddlelike wings. None of them can fly.

All birds, however, have feathers, which no other living animal has, though paleontologists have found fossilized remains of a few dinosaurs and other reptiles—probably the ancestors of birds—that appear to have had feathers. Birds are feathered, warm-blooded animals with backbones. They have two legs. Whether they fly or not, all have a pair of wings corresponding to the arms or the front legs of many other animals. A beak takes the place of a jaw with teeth. All birds lay eggs. Most of them build a nest in which they care for the eggs and the young birds.

## MAMMALS

Despite their size differences, the great blue whale and the pygmy shrew have something in common: they are both members of the warm-blooded, air-breathing class of vertebrate animals known as Mammalia, or mammals. In many ways mammals are the most highly developed of all creatures.

The term mammal explains one important way in which creatures in this class are set apart from other animals. It comes from the Latin *mamma*, which means "breast." Every female mammal has special glands, mammae, that secrete milk. The females of all but the most primitive mammalian species are viviparous. This means they bear their young alive. The young are then fed with milk until they have grown enough to get food for themselves.

*A dog nurses her 12 puppies in Beijing, China.* **AFP/Getty Images**

Hair is a typical mammalian feature. In many whales, however, it exists only in the fetal stages of development. Another basic trait of mammals is their highly developed brains—the most complex known. Particularly well developed is their cerebrum, the part of the brain that controls memory and learning. The mammalian brain enables the young to learn from the experience of their elders.

72

# OUR CLOSEST RELATIVE, THE CHIMPANZEE

The best studied of the great apes, the chimpanzee, is considered by most authorities to be the closest living relative to humans.

*A chimpanzee cradles her newborn.* **AFP/Getty Images**

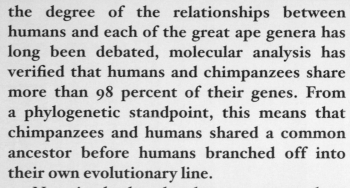

the degree of the relationships between humans and each of the great ape genera has long been debated, molecular analysis has verified that humans and chimpanzees share more than 98 percent of their genes. From a phylogenetic standpoint, this means that chimpanzees and humans shared a common ancestor before humans branched off into their own evolutionary line.

No animal other than humans uses tools as effectively as the chimpanzee. Highly intelligent and resourceful, they use sticks to extract termites from the termites' nest and to pull down branches that are beyond their reach. They use leaves to clean their bodies and as sponges to pick up drinking water from holes in tree trunks. In addition, they often modify objects to suit their purpose—for example, stripping a twig of its leaves before plunging it into an anthill. Studies suggest that the use of tools is not instinctive but rather is learned by juveniles through observation and imitation of adults.

Since the young mammal is dependent on its mother for nourishment, a period of learning is possible. This in turn has brought about a degree of behavioral adaptability unknown in any other group of organisms. Whales, seals, and dogs are among the most intelligent mammals, but monkeys, apes, and humans are the most intelligent of all.

People have always been fascinated by animals. Ancient humans observed animals closely, partly out of curiosity but primarily because early human survival depended to a great extent on knowledge of animal behavior. Whether hunting wild game, keeping domesticated animals, or escaping a predator, success required intimate knowledge of an animal's habits. Today, most people have a less practical interest in observing animals; they simply enjoy the antics and activities of pets, of animals in zoos, and of wildlife.

Even today, however, the study of animals and their habits is of considerable importance. For example, in Britain, research on the social organization and ranging patterns of badgers has helped reduce the spread of tuberculosis among cattle. In Sweden, where collisions involving moose are among the most common traffic accidents in rural areas, studies of moose behavior have yielded ways of keeping them off the roads. In addition, investigations of the foraging of insect pollinators, such as honeybees, have led to

impressive increases in agricultural crop yields throughout the world.

Of course, people also study animals in order to learn about themselves. Humans are a very recent product of the evolution of animals, and it is apparent that the behavior of some creatures—particularly those with whom we share an evolutionary history—is not so very different from human behavior. Undoubtedly there remains much yet to discover about the staggeringly diverse world of animals and about the relationship of humans to other animal species.

**archaea** Any of a group of single-celled prokaryotic organisms that have distinct molecular characteristics separating them from bacteria as well as from eukaryotes.

**arthropod** Any of a phylum of animals without backbones (as insects, arachnids, and crustaceans) having a segmented body, jointed limbs, and a shell of chitin that is shed periodically.

**bacterium** Any of a group of single-celled microorganisms that live in soil, water, organic matter, or the bodies of plants and animals.

**carnivore** A flesh-eating animal.

**chordate** Any of a major group of animals (as vertebrates and tunicates) having at least at some stage of development a flexible rod of cells forming a support along the back, a central nervous system located in the back, and openings for water to pass over the gills.

**class** A major category in biological classification that is above the order and below the phylum.

**domain** The highest taxonomic category in biological classification ranking above the kingdom.

**ectoderm** The outermost of the three basic layers of an embryo from which skin, nerves, and certain other structures develop.

**endoderm** The inner layer of cells of an animal (as a jellyfish or hydra) whose body is composed of two layers of cells.

**family** A group of related plants or animals ranking in biological classification above a genus and below an order.

**genus** A category of classification in biology that ranks between the family and the species, and contains related species.

**herbivore** A plant-eating animal.

**kingdom** A major category in the scientific classification of living things that ranks above the phylum and is the highest and broadest group.

**mesoderm** The middle layer of cells of an embryonic animal from which most of the muscular, skeletal, and connective tissues develop.

**metazoan** Any of the great group of animals with a body composed of cells forming tissues and organs.

**mollusk** Any of a large phylum of invertebrate animals (as snails, clams, and octopuses) with a soft body lacking segments and usually enclosed in a shell containing calcium.

**order** A category of taxonomic classification ranking above the family and below the class.

**protozoan** Any of a phylum or group of tiny, animal-like organisms that are not divided into cells and have varied structure and physiology and often complicated life cycles.

**phylogenetic** Based on natural evolutionary relationships.

**phylum** A primary category in biological taxonomy that ranks above the class and below the kingdom.

**species** A category of living things that ranks below a genus, is made up of related individuals able to produce fertile offspring, and is identified by a two-part scientific name.

Canadian Wildlife Federation (CWF)
350 Michael Cowpland Drive
Kanata, ON K2M 2W1
Canada
(800) 563-9453
Web site: http://www.cwf-fcf.org
The CWF educates the Canadian public on
   issues of wildlife conservation through
   its advocacy efforts, publications, and
   programs.

National Wildlife Federation (NWF)
11100 Wildlife Center Drive
Reston, VA 20190
(800) 822-9919
Web site: http://www.nwf.org
The NWF has initiated a number of conservation efforts designed to protect wildlife
   and natural resources throughout the
   United States. It inspires public interest through its environmental education
   efforts and activity guides.

San Diego Zoo
2920 Zoo Drive
San Diego, CA 92101
(619) 231-1515
Web site: http://www.sandiegozoo.org
The San Diego Zoo gives visitors access

to over 4,000 animals from across the globe. Committed to conservation efforts, its Institute for Conservation Research uses scientific innovation to preserve the planet's biodiversity.

Toronto Zoo
361A Old Finch Avenue
Toronto, ON M1B 5K7
Canada
(416) 392-5929
Web site: http://www.torontozoo.com
With over 5,000 animals, the Toronto Zoo
    is one of the largest in the world. In addi-
    tion to exploring its diverse collection
    of species as visitors, the public can take
    advantage of one of its many educational
    programs or camps.

World Wildlife Fund (WWF)
U.S. Headquarters
1250 24th Street NW
P.O. Box 97180
Washington, DC 20090
(202) 293-4800
Web site: http://www.worldwildlife.org
The WWF is a global organization dedi-
    cated to protecting the planet's various
    life forms. It is noted for scientific

research and advocacy initiatives on a host of conservation-related topics, with a special emphasis on wildlife and natural habitats.

Zoological Association of America (ZAA)
P.O. Box 511275
Punta Gorda, FL 33951
(941) 621-2021
Web site: http://www.zaoa.org
The ZAA and its members promote research and interest in wildlife and conservation efforts in order to ensure the protection of all privately- and publicly-owned animals.

## WEB SITES

Due to the changing nature of Internet links, Rosen Educational Services has developed an online list of Web sites related to the subject of this book. This site is updated regularly. Please use this link to access the list:

http://www.rosenlinks.com/biol/anim

Damron, W.S. *Introduction to Animal Science*, 4th ed. (Pearson, 2009).

Farndon, John. *Wildlife Atlas* (Reader's Digest, 2002).

Hare, Tony. *Animal Habitats: Discovering How Animals Live in the Wild* (Facts on File, 2001).

Lock, David. *Animals at Home* (DK, 2007).

Macdonald, D.W., ed. *The Princeton Encyclopedia of Mammals* (Princeton University Press, 2009).

McGhee, Karen, and McKay, George. *Encyclopedia of Animals* (National Geographic, 2007).

Minelli, Alessandro, and Mannucci, Maria Pia. *Surviving: How Animals Adapt to Their Environments* (Firefly, 2009).

Nelson, J.S. *Fishes of the World*, 4th ed. (Wiley, 2006).

Rylant, Cynthia, and Davis, Lambert. *The Journey: Stories of Migration* (Blue Sky Press, 2006).

Sibley, D.A. *The Sibley Guide to Bird Life & Behavior* (Knopf, 2009).

Taylor, Barbara. *1,000 Fascinating Animal Facts* (Lorenz, 2008).

Zweifel, R.G., and Cogger, H.G., eds. *Encyclopedia of Reptiles and Amphibians*, 2nd ed. (Academic Press, 1998).

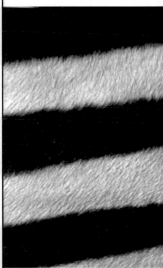
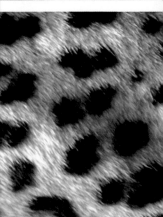

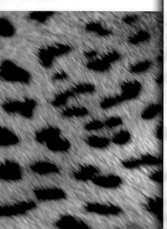